D1528693

Children of the World

Vietnam

For a free color catalog describing Gareth Stevens' list of high-quality children's books, call 1-800-341-3569 (USA) or 1-800-461-9120 (Canada).

For their help in the preparation of *Children of the World: Vietnam*, the writer and editor gratefully thank Boi Ngoc Nguyen of Shorewood, Wisconsin, and all the children of Vietnam.

All photographs are by Vu Viet Dung except those on pages 8-9, 20, 36, 38, 40, 43 (both), 45, and 46-47, all by Hong-Phong Pho.

Flag illustration on page 48, © Flag Research Center.

Library of Congress Cataloging-in-Publication Data

Norland, Patricia.
    Vietnam / written by Patricia Norland ; photography by Vu Viet Dung.
       p. cm. — (Children of the world)
    Includes bibliographical references and index.
    Summary: Presents the life of an eleven-year-old girl and her family in Vietnam, describing her home and school
activities and discussing the history, geography, ethnic composition, languages, culture, and other aspects of her country.
    ISBN 0-8368-0230-6
    1. Vietnam—Juvenile literature. 2. Children—Vietnam—Juvenile literature. [1. Vietnam. 2. Family life—Vietnam.]
I. Vu, Viet Dung. II. Title. III. Series.
DS556.3.N67 1991
959.704'4—dc20
                                            89-43178

A Gareth Stevens Children's Books edition

Edited, designed, and produced by
Gareth Stevens Children's Books
1555 North RiverCenter Drive, Suite 201
Milwaukee, Wisconsin 53212, USA

Series editor: Valerie Weber
Editor: Patricia Lantier-Sampon
Research editor: John D. Rateliff
Designer: Sabine Huschke
Map design: Sheri Gibbs

Printed in the United States of America

1 2 3 4 5 6 7 8 9 97 96 95 94 93 92 91

Children of the World
Vietnam

Text by Patricia Norland
Photography by Vu Viet Dung

Gareth Stevens Children's Books
MILWAUKEE

. . . a note about *Children of the World*:

The children of the world live in fishing towns, Arctic regions, and urban centers, on islands and in mountain valleys, on sheep ranches and fruit farms. This series follows one child in each country through the pattern of his or her life. Candid photographs show the children with their families, at school, at play, and in their communities. The text describes the dreams of the children and, often through their own words, tells how they see themselves and their lives.

Each book also explores events that are unique to the country in which the child lives, including festivals, religious ceremonies, and national holidays. The *Children of the World* series does more than tell about foreign countries. It introduces the children of each country and shows readers what it is like to be a child in that country.

Children of the World includes the following published and soon-to-be-published titles:

Argentina	El Salvador	Jordan	South Africa
Australia	Finland	Kenya	South Korea
Belize	France	Malaysia	Spain
Bhutan	Greece	Mexico	Sweden
Bolivia	Guatemala	Nepal	Tanzania
Brazil	Honduras	New Zealand	Thailand
Burma (Myanmar)	Hong Kong	Nicaragua	Turkey
Canada	Hungary	Nigeria	USSR
China	India	Panama	Vietnam
Costa Rica	Indonesia	Peru	West Germany
Cuba	Ireland	Philippines	Yugoslavia
Czechoslovakia	Italy	Poland	Zambia
Egypt	Japan	Singapore	

. . . and about *Vietnam*:

Ho thi Kim Chau is an eleven-year-old girl who lives with her family in a tiny village outside of Ho Chi Minh City in Vietnam. She helps with household chores, tends the family animals, and enjoys playing games with her friends when she has time to spare. Kim Chau likes to visit the big city, which is ten miles away, but she is really a country girl at heart.

To enhance this book's value in libraries and classrooms, comprehensive reference sections include up-to-date information about Vietnam's geography, demographics, language, currency, education, culture, industry, and natural resources. *Vietnam* also features glossaries of English and Vietnamese terms, a bibliography, research projects and activities, and discussions of such subjects as Hanoi, the country's history, language, political system, and ethnic and religious composition.

The living conditions and experiences of children in Vietnam vary according to economic, environmental, and ethnic circumstances. The reference sections help bring to life for young readers the diversity and richness of the culture and heritage of Vietnam. Of particular interest are discussions of the Vietnam War and the country's current political situation, the richness of its religious customs, and its long and exciting history.

CONTENTS

LIVING IN VIETNAM:
Chau, a Country Girl near the City

Ho thi Kim Chau is 11 years old and lives with her family in the tiny village of Binh Quoi Tay, ten miles (16 km) west of Ho Chi Minh City. For centuries, her ancestors have lived in or near the big city, which used to be called Saigon. Chau's family includes her father, Ho Van Nho, her mother, Nguyen thi Muoi, and two younger sisters, Loan and Oanh.

The small village Chau calls home seems far away from the bustle of the big city. But Chau is grateful for the beautiful peace and quiet of the Binh Thanh district. Not only are there several family pets to enjoy, but also many games to play, friends to see, and relatives to visit.

As a visitor leaves Ho Chi Minh City and approaches Chau's village, crowded city dwellings and paved roads give way to homes built far apart and rough pathways among bright green rice fields. Chau's village is a series of homes with gardens and fields stretching out between them.

Eleven-year-old Ho thi Kim Chau, like four-fifths of Vietnam's population, lives in the countryside. Her home is in the tiny village of Binh Quoi Tay. ▶

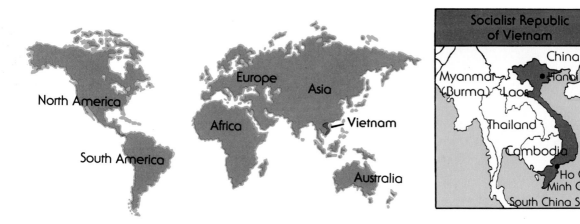

6

Vietnam is a rice-growing nation; planting rice is hard, back-breaking work.

Kim Chau and Her Family

During the day, Kim Chau's father, Nho, tends the garden that surrounds the house and feeds the family's many chickens and ducks. Three nights a week, he is also a guard in a paper factory. He rides his bicycle to the factory, which is about four miles (6 km) from home. Nho has an easygoing personality; he and Chau's mother like to relax by listening to radio programs or music on his battery-powered cassette recorder.

Nguyen thi Muoi, Chau's mother, is a homemaker. She takes care of Chau and her sisters, sews clothes for the family, goes to the market two or three times a week, and helps Nho do the family gardening.

Nho's parents work as gardeners and live just 200 yards (183 m) away. Muoi's parents are carpenters. They live some distance away in the Thu Duc district. To visit them, the family has to cross the Saigon River in a *sampan*, a shallow wooden boat.

The three generations of Chau's family often gather at her house for meals. Chau and her sisters enjoy playing with their grandparents.

Many Vietnamese travel along the rivers and streams of their country in boats called *sampans*.

Chau helps her mother organize the dishes after washing them.

◀ Chau's mother often needs the help of her daughters to complete all the household chores.

In Vietnam, last names are first, and first names are last! In Ho thi Kim Chau's name, Ho is the family name of Chau's father. Chau is her first name. Names also have meanings: Chau means "gemstone"; Loan is the word for the phoenix, a legendary bird; and Oanh is the word for a common bird, the oriole. Muoi means "ten" in Vietnamese, although Chau's mother is the ninth child in her family. By tradition, especially in southern Vietnam, the father is considered number one. For this reason, the first child is often named number two.

Chau's earliest memory is of her mother, the most beautiful and valuable person in the world to her. Since Chau wants to be like her mother, she does all the things Muoi asks her to do. Most Vietnamese children are taught at a very young age to honor and respect their elders. Muoi spends more time with the children than Nho, and she disciplines them more often. This is common in Vietnamese families.

13

Home: A Quiet Haven

Chau lives in the Binh Thanh district. Her parents built their two-room house in 1983 on some land that belonged to Nho's parents. Palm and eucalyptus trees stand between the house and the Saigon River, 300 yards (274 m) behind the house. Sugarcane and cassava grow in the fields lining the property. To get to the main road, Chau walks a little more than one mile (2 km) along a narrow, rough path. Coconut and eucalyptus trees and bamboo shade her from the hot sun.

A dozen areca palm trees stand in front of Chau's house while sugarcane stalks border one side and the back. The house has two rooms with clay floors and a tiled roof. Tightly woven straw forms both the inner and outer walls of the dwelling. The larger room is a living area, bedroom, and sewing area, all in one. The smaller room serves as a kitchen and dining room. Wood used for cooking is piled next to the fireplace, and a hammock swings gently in one corner of the kitchen.

Chau's house is much larger than the cramped quarters shared by families living in nearby Ho Chi Minh City. ▶

While Chau and Loan play in the hammock, their grandfather prefers to relax quietly.

Chau helps her sisters do their homework.

When she is not wearing her elegant *ao dai*, Chau's grandmother dresses in *ao baba*, loose-fitting pajamas ▶

The fields, river, and garden around Chau's house make it calm and quiet, which is good for studying. Chau spends many hours doing lessons in the early morning hours. The soft and peaceful noises outside help her concentrate.

Chau also works hard at sewing in her spare time. She would like to sew as well as her mother does. Maybe one day soon she will learn to make an *ao dai*, a traditional outfit worn by many Vietnamese women. An ao dai has two pieces — a long dress worn over a pair of very loose pants. Chau's grandmother, Nho's mother, has a silk ao dai that she wears on special days or for special events. Chau thinks her grandmother looks very elegant and regal in her traditional Vietnamese clothing.

Daily Chores and Tasty Treats

Chau gets up at 6:00 a.m. each morning. After washing and dressing, she chops wood and helps her mother start a fire to cook rice. At every meal, Chau's family eats rice, the most common food in Vietnam. Breakfast is boiled rice with meat or fish cooked in fish sauce or fish paste. The meal almost always includes bananas.

Vietnamese eat with either large soup spoons or chopsticks.

Nho hauls water from the river with a yoke and two pails slung across his shoulders.

Right: Chau uses a handmade broom to sweep the kitchen area. Metal pans and woven baskets hang on the kitchen wall.

After breakfast, Chau sweeps the yard and feeds the chickens and ducks. Sometimes her mother may ask her to buy something from the tiny store inside a neighbor's house. This little store carries many necessary household items, such as sugar, salt, and matches. Children can also purchase candy and other special treats here.

The water that Chau's family uses comes from the Saigon River. Chau's father carries water from the river in giant pails, two at a time. River water is then stored in a 50-gallon (190-L) barrel beside the house. This water must be boiled before it is safe for drinking. But water for bathing and for watering the garden can be used directly from the barrel.

Fishing is an important industry throughout Vietnam, which has a very long coastline. Some families make their homes on the fishing boats.

At about 8:00 a.m. each morning, after her chores are completed, Chau begins her schoolwork. Later, she helps her mother fix lunch. Two days a week, Chau takes care of her sisters so Muoi can bicycle the two miles (3.2 km) to the market. Chau and her sisters also help their mother do the laundry in buckets at the back of the house. Then they hang the wet clothes out in the yard to dry.

Chau's mother does most of her shopping at the Thanh Da market, which lies a short distance from her own village. She finds all kinds of essential household goods and tasty foods there. Many fruits in Vietnam, such as *vu sua*, or milk apple, are hard to find in other parts of the world. *Buoi*, or *pomelo*, is a grapefruit, but bigger and sweeter than the ones usually found in North America. *Chom chom*, also known as *rambutan*, has a sweet and juicy taste. *Xoai*, or mango, is one of the country's tastiest fruits. *Sau rieng*, a football-sized fruit also called *durian*, has a terrible smell. But many people still like its soft, tangy, yellow sections.

Many vendors at the Thanh Da market arrange their fruits and vegetables under an umbrella to protect them from the hot sun.

Favorite Pets and Pastimes

Chau and her family have several pets. The dogs are named Va, which means "spotted," and Muc, which means "black." Their cat has no name. Chau's favorite pets are the ducks, and she happily brings leftover food to twenty of them each day.

In her spare time, Chau plays with two girlfriends, Nga and My, who live nearby. They come to the house to talk, jump rope, or play house. Hung, an 11-year-old boy, also lives nearby and sometimes joins them. After an early dinner, Chau goes to bed at 7:00 p.m. The whole family goes to bed early because the house has kerosene lamps but no electricity.

Obviously, Chau's family does not have a television set or a telephone either. These luxuries are expensive and rather scarce in the rural areas of the country. To watch television, Chau goes to a neighbor's house. She likes to watch traditional theater plays and *cai luong*, a popular form of musical soap opera. To see movies or to visit the zoo, Chau and her family must travel to Ho Chi Minh City.

Chau performs many chores around the house and yard. She really enjoys feeding the ducks!

Playing with her friends makes Chau happy.

Va keeps Kim Chau and her sisters company as they play quietly together.

Chau's School Day

Chau and her family eat lunch at 11:00 a.m. so that she is ready to walk to school by 11:30 a.m. School is more than a mile (1.6 km) away. It takes Chau 45 minutes to walk there. Friends join her for the daily hike. During the rainy season, between April and October, walking to school is difficult because the roads are so muddy.

Most Vietnamese children attend the free schooling provided by the Communist government. Because they are needed to help out at home, children sometimes must miss many days at school or stop attending altogether. Despite these breaks in their schooling, it is estimated that 94% of all Vietnamese people can read and write.

Students wear school uniforms provided by their families. Chau and the other girls wear white shirts and blue skirts or blue pants. The boys wear blue pants and white shirts.

Chau's six-year-old sister, Loan, is in first grade. Her other sister, Oanh, is four and stays at home. She will start school next year.

◀ The rice paddy on Chau's way to school is ready for harvest. The rice grains, hidden by the tall leaves, give off a delicate, sweet smell.

Chau complements her school uniform with a hat to help protect her from the sun's harsh midday heat.

Chau's two-story school is bigger and more modern than most school buildings in rural Vietnam.

Chau attends a public primary and secondary school. There are 623 students and 27 teachers, but only seven classrooms! Classes are crowded because there are so many young people in Vietnam and because the government has little money for building schools and buying school supplies. To make it possible for all students to attend classes, there are two separate school sessions. Morning students attend from 7:30 to 11:30 a.m., while afternoon students go from 1:00 to 4:30 p.m. There are 33 boys and girls in Chau's afternoon class.

Chau's school is in session five days a week. There are no classes on Thursdays or Sundays. The school year lasts nine months, with a three-month break in June, July, and August. Some parents pay for their children to attend a private summer school session so that their education can continue all year. Chau's parents cannot afford summer school, so Chau remains at home during this time. She spends her vacation caring for the animals, helping her mother with household chores, and playing games with her friends.

Teachers are well respected in Vietnam, even though they get very little pay.

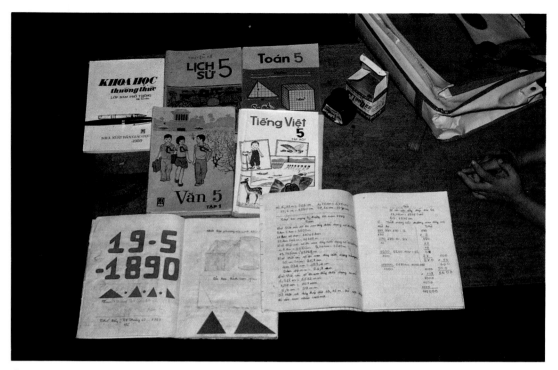

Chau has different schoolbooks for her classes in literature, science, history, and mathematics. Students often use fountain pens as well as ball-point pens.

Chau and her school friends talk and laugh together during a break in the afternoon.

Chau takes many courses during the school day. Her classes include mathematics, reading, history, drawing, Vietnamese literature, practical science, manual work, and morals. Practical science teaches Chau the value of good personal hygiene. In her manual work class, she learns how to raise and care for animals, while the class on morals teaches her to be a good citizen. But Chau's favorite class is reading. She likes to read aloud and especially enjoys Vietnamese legends and fairy tales.

Vietnamese is a tonal language. This means that words spelled the same way can be pronounced as many as six different ways. Each way gives the word a different meaning. Accent marks above or below each word tell how the word is pronounced. Next year, in sixth grade, Chau will decide what foreign language to learn in addition to her native language. Her choices include English, which is important as an international language; French, since France used to rule Vietnam and many older Vietnamese still use it; and Russian, the language of the Soviets, who have supplied Vietnam with oil, grain, and some basic technology.

Chau, fourth from left in the front row, stands with her teacher and the rest of her afternoon class.

Games to Play

A drum at school announces recess at 2:30 p.m. For ten minutes, students do gymnastics to the beat of the drum. Government officials at every level encourage young children to be physically fit. The remaining 20 minutes are free playtime. Chau and her friends like to jump rope. They call it *skip* or *hop*, and have contests to see who can skip the longest. Boys often play hide-and-seek or spin tops.

Vietnamese children also like to play jacks. But they don't have a rubber ball or metal jacks, since these items are both hard to find and very expensive. So they use a lime as a ball and chopsticks, whole or broken into pieces, as jacks. Another popular game uses a plastic toy with feathers, like a badminton birdie. The players kick the birdie quickly, trying to keep it from hitting the ground.

The girls take on the boys in a tug of war. Instead of using a rope, team members each hang on to the waist of the person in front of them. Team leaders clasp hands, and then each side pulls!

The Vietnamese people believe strongly in the importance of keeping physically fit.

Right: Few village homes have running water. These schoolboys can easily help draw water.

31

Downtown Ho Chi Minh City during Tet: Vendors sell festive flowers alongside a cyclo stand.

In and around Ho Chi Minh City

Chau and her family enjoy visiting Ho Chi Minh City, a major city in southern Vietnam. A busy place with shady trees and pretty boulevards, it is a curious mixture of 19th-century French architecture, Japanese motorbikes, and modern buildings. Chau likes to look at the tamarind trees that have red-striped yellow flowers and grow throughout the area. Bougainvillea, a woody vine found in tropical countries, also adds bright purple and red splashes of color to the bustling city.

Ho Chi Minh City's streets are packed with traffic, most of it on two wheels! Cars are rare in Vietnam, but many people ride on bicycles, motorbikes, or on three-wheeled bikes called cyclos. Chau thinks that riding a bicycle in this city is scary at first because it is easy to be swept away by the traffic. On many street corners, bicycle mechanics set up instant repair shops. With only a few tools, they can quickly fix flat tires and other bicycle parts.

Cyclos are the taxis of Vietnam. The drivers pedal people and goods around town!

Ho Chi Minh City's zoo was originally built by the French.

Visiting the City and the Zoo

Going to the zoo in Ho Chi Minh City is an all-day activity. Chau and her family rent two cyclos, each with a large seat attached to the frame. Ho Chi Minh City takes more than 90 minutes to reach by cyclo.

At the zoo, the girls buy balloons and try to see as many animals as they can. They watch the elephants eat straw and see the black panther pace in his cage. They giggle at the monkeys. Vibrant colors and beautiful tropical flowers are everywhere.

Chau's father buys coconuts at the zoo. The vendor chops a hole in the top of each coconut and pops a straw into it. The girls sip the sweet, clear juice inside.

At the end of an afternoon of walking through the zoo, the girls are hungry. The family stops to eat noodle soup, called *pho*. Each person's bowl of soup costs less than 25 cents.

In the past, elephants carried commanding officers into battle! They also pulled heavy loads.

After the zoo, the family heads toward the main market. The Ben Thanh market is a hangarlike structure filled with narrow stalls and unusual smells. Odors from tropical fruits, fresh fish, and simmering noodle soup mix with other spicy smells. Hundreds of merchants squat behind piles of food or other goods. While most vendors speak Vietnamese, some call out in English to foreigners who are shopping: "Best price, here!" or "Cheap, very cheap!"

One section of the market is devoted to dishware and chinaware imported from China, Taiwan, and Hong Kong. Another area has stalls filled with woven straw goods, such as hats and baskets. Many people crowd around the stand where thermal bottles from China are sold. A thermal bottle, while expensive, is vital for a tea-drinking people such as the Vietnamese. Trinkets, toy gadgets, and colorful calendars are sold near the entrances to the Ben Thanh market. Chau's mother buys only what she can't find at the market near their home.

During Tet, people can buy fruit and flower baskets made out of dough! ▶

Alongside sidewalk restaurants, women sort rice and beans used to make rice cakes.

A statue of the Virgin Mary dominates the scene in front of Notre Dame Cathedral.

On the way out of the city, the family stops to look at Notre Dame Cathedral. This beautiful structure, built by the French who colonized Vietnam, is located just a short distance from downtown. About 10% of southern Vietnamese are Roman Catholics, and at Sunday morning masses, Notre Dame is crowded with many people, young and old alike. This cathedral has one of Ho Chi Minh City's most elegant and imposing facades jutting high above the surrounding buildings, and it is considered one of the city's most colorful sights. During the Christmas season, people can buy Christmas cards just across the street from the cathedral.

The beautiful city named after Ho Chi Minh is hectic and exciting at almost any time of the day or night. The people seem full of energy for their day's work. Chau and her family have fun just being a part of the crowd and looking at all the vivid colors and interesting sights.

The area around Notre Dame Cathedral, especially during Tet, is filled with swirling crowds on foot, on motorcycles, and in cars.

Snacks and Specialties

Back in the peaceful quiet of home, Chau sometimes indulges in her favorite foods and treats. Her favorite dishes include different kinds of meat. For a snack, she likes to eat corn on the cob, which children call "playing the harmonica." Another favorite snack is sticky rice steamed in coconut milk. Usually everyone at home drinks plain boiled water, but Chau's favorite drink is iced lemonade, called *nuoc chanh*.

When Chau is sick, her mother makes plain soup made of boiled rice. This is supposed to help her feel better. Muoi also encourages Chau to drink sweetened condensed milk and eat fresh oranges.

Meat and fish dishes in Vietnam are often served with a special fish sauce called *nuoc mam*. Chau's family makes its own nuoc mam. Her father mixes layers of tiny fish and salt in a barrel and allows the ingredients to stand undisturbed for a month or longer. A liquid from the decomposing fish mixes with the salt and drains from the bottom of the barrel. Some people add crushed garlic, lemon juice, sugar, and hot peppers. Vietnam sells this tangy sauce to many countries.

Women sell hunks of fresh fish just outside the Ben Thanh market.

40

Vietnamese cuisine requires many fresh ingredients and careful preparation.

Customs and Festivals

The Vietnamese people have many different religious customs. For example, an altar to Chau's ancestors stands in the middle of the family's larger room. The Hos practice the cult of the ancestors and pay respect to close family members who have died. Every year, on the anniversaries of their relatives' deaths, family and friends gather together. Guests place food and drink on the altar. Ancestor worshipers believe that the dead will come to share the elaborate meal.

Most Vietnamese people do not celebrate birthdays. On her first birthday, Chau's family followed another custom, *thoi noi* — the child's leaving the cradle. Chau sat in the middle of a large room. Her parents put several items around her in a circle. Each item symbolized what Chau might become as an adult.

Scissors represented Chau's becoming a tailor. A ruler indicated she might become a teacher. A piece of soil suggested she might be a farmer. A pen predicted she might be a scholar. The first item Chau touched indicated what she might become later in life. Chau's hand first landed on the scissors.

Chau and her sisters watch as their father holds an incense stick while praying at the family altar.

Throughout Vietnam, families practice the cult of the ancestors. Family members place fruit, rice, and vegetables on the altar to share with deceased relatives.

Right: The photo of a family ancestor hangs above a family altar.

During Tet, firecrackers tied to a tree explode with sharp sounds and puffs of smoke.

Tet

Tet, a celebration of the Vietnamese New Year, is the most important time of year for Chau and her family. This lunar New Year festival lasts for several days and marks the transition from the old to the new year and the birth of spring.

During Tet, the Ho family visits a pagoda or temple in Ho Chi Minh City to pray for a happy new year. They ask for luck, good fortune, and health for themselves and their relatives. At the festival, Chau and her sisters light firecrackers to scare away evil spirits that may be left over from the old year.

Chau and her family attend several theatrical presentations during the celebration. They also watch boxing contests, dancing events, and traditional musical groups. The week offers many valuable opportunities for Chau to learn more about her native culture and to share new experiences with the people she loves most. But when Tet festivities in Ho Chi Minh City finally end, Chau eagerly looks toward Binh Quoi Tay. Although the big city has plenty of exciting sights, she is a country girl at heart. Ho thi Kim Chau is happy to go home.

During Tet, many firecrackers of different sizes are often strung together. The firecrackers go off in a chain reaction when someone lights one end of the group.

During Tet, each village has its own festival day. This particular scene took place in the village of Dong Ky, in northern Vietnam.

FOR YOUR INFORMATION: Vietnam

Official Name: Cong Hoa Xa Hoi Chu Nghia Viet Nam
(kong wah zah hoy chu nwee VEE-et nahm)
Socialist Republic of Vietnam

Capital: Hanoi

History

The First Vietnamese

Someone has said that Vietnam and China are as close as lips and teeth. This has always been true and still holds true today. In fact, the first people who could be called Vietnamese probably came from China. Warring Chinese pushed these people south, forcing them to leave their homes in southern China in about 3000 BC. These Vietnamese gradually moved down the western shore of the South China Sea. Where the coastland was fertile, they farmed. Where the coastland was mountainous, they lived by hunting and fishing. In northern Vietnam, people began to farm in the Red River delta as early as 600 BC. Much later, about AD 600, they settled in the Mekong River delta in the south. Rice and other crops grew well in these wet lowlands.

Large crowds of people fill the streets of Hanoi during most of the day and night.

The Chinese eventually became interested in this narrow country with its wide rivers, warm climate, and new language and culture. A Chinese general named Trieu Da marched into Vietnam with his army in about 200 BC. In the century that followed, the Chinese conquered the north, and the Vietnamese people became little more than servants. They gave part of each crop to the local Chinese lord, who protected them from bandits and other warlords. The Chinese believed that their society was the best in the world and they spent a lot of time imposing their customs on the Vietnamese people. The Chinese refused to learn Vietnamese, outlawed local customs, and relied solely on Chinese religion, philosophy, government, and technology.

The Vietnamese often revolted against the Chinese. In AD 40, for example, two brave Vietnamese sisters named Trung created a small, independent northern state that lasted two years. Their tiny nation was eventually overwhelmed by Chinese forces, and the sisters flung themselves into a river rather than be captured.

More uprisings against the Chinese followed. In about AD 250, a Vietnamese group led by a woman named Trieu Au held off Chinese soldiers for six months before she, too, chose suicide over capture. Considered the Joan of Arc of Vietnam, Trieu Au wore gold armor, rode elephants, and led a thousand men into battle. She died at the age of 23. There are still temples to Trieu Au and the Trung sisters in Vietnam. They are worshiped as national goddesses. Later, in about AD 550, a man of Chinese ancestry named Ly Bon led Vietnamese rebels into northern mountains, where their control throughout the surrounding countryside lasted more than 50 years.

Not until AD 939 were all Chinese finally chased north, out of the country. A Vietnamese mandarin named Ngo Quyen united several small, warring Vietnamese armies, expelled the Chinese, and declared himself emperor.

For the next 600 years, Vietnam saw few outsiders. But on three separate occasions in the 13th century, brave Vietnamese defeated huge Mongolian armies attempting to enter Vietnam. In addition, in 1407, the Chinese invaded once again. This time, they stayed for only about ten years. The Vietnamese people by then had rebuilt their own culture, and it was clear to the Chinese that they would have to fight the Vietnamese constantly. In 1428, both countries signed a treaty declaring Vietnam an independent nation.

A few years later, the Vietnamese emperor Le Thanh Ton introduced many reforms. Peasants received some protection against landlords, the arts were encouraged, and education spread into rural areas. Laws and school lessons were discussed in Vietnamese, but they had to be written in Chinese script since no written Vietnamese language had been developed yet.

By 1620, the northern half of today's Vietnam was thickly populated. A second government sprang up in Hue, which is hundreds of miles south of Hanoi, the capital of the north. The Nguyen family operated a separate kingdom there for more than 100 years and refused obedience to the ruling Trinhs in Hanoi.

Vietnam's leaders at the time were top civil and military officials from the ruling class known as mandarins. They studied for years in order to pass hard examinations that allowed them to conduct affairs for the emperor. Until the arrival of Westerners, mandarins ran the country, while emperor after emperor came and went.

The French Arrive

That changed with the arrival of Alexandre de Rhodes. He was a French missionary, one of the first Westerners to visit Vietnam. In 1627, he created a written Vietnamese alphabet called *quoc ngu*. This alphabet helped the Catholic church convert the Vietnamese people — now they could read the Bible and become Christians. Written language also increased the influence of French explorers and traders since they no longer had to deal with the Vietnamese solely in person; they could write to them instead.

The French came to Vietnam during a time when there was a lot of internal fighting over territory. French missionaries usually backed the stronger side. When that side won, Christianity then gained many converts. By 1799, France had enough influence to help a man named Gia Long become the ruler of Vietnam. In exchange, the French demanded special favors. They wanted to get rich by being the only Europeans trading with Vietnam. Backing their decisions with weapons and soldiers, the traders soon were running much of the country. By the end of the 19th century, the French had found an excuse to rule all of Vietnam.

The Vietnamese emperor at the time was named Tu Duc. He came to the throne in 1847, vowing to erase Christianity in his country. This angered the French, who captured the large southern city of Saigon in 1861 and took control of the country from Tu Duc the next year. Once in control of Vietnam, overrunning neighboring Cambodia and Laos was easy. By 1887, French forces had gained control of all three countries. The area became known as the colony of French Indochina.

Foreign rule did not agree with the Vietnamese. It made no difference that they had no guns and few other weapons; they still staged hundreds of small rebellions. But the French usually rounded up the rebellious men and women and quickly killed them, thereby preventing any native leaders from emerging. A leader, however, eventually did emerge.

Ho Chi Minh, the Father of Modern Vietnam

Ho Chi Minh's real name was Nguyen Tat Thanh. He was born on May 19, 1890, in a poor farming village in central Vietnam. He changed his name at first to Nguyen Ai Quoc, or "Nguyen the Patriot," and studied to become a schoolteacher. As a young man, he roamed the world, working as a seaman and a laborer. He even stayed briefly in New York City, where he worked in a hotel restaurant washing dishes and waiting on tables!

The man by then called Ho Chi Minh, or "Bringer of Enlightenment," formed his political ideas in Paris, where he studied from 1941 to 1945. He admired French culture, but not when it suppressed Vietnam's own culture. He believed that the French were taking all the wealth out of his land and leaving the Vietnamese people poor and ill-educated. His lifelong goal was the independence of Vietnam.

Traveling to China, he organized the Indochinese Communist party in 1930. After World War II broke out in 1939, he worked his way back into Vietnam and led a small band of soldiers who hid in the northern mountains. Living in damp caves, they fought the Japanese, who had marched into Vietnam to throw the French out in 1941. After World War II, the French resumed control of Southeast Asia. They had ruled Vietnam for over 80 years and believed that it belonged to them. Such a belief is called colonialism.

In late 1945, Ho Chi Minh entered Hanoi, the nation's capital. He declared Vietnam independent and said he was the country's president. Ho's declaration of independence was copied from that of the United States, but many Vietnamese were too busy trying to survive to take much notice.

War in Indochina

The French paid no attention, either. Relations between Ho's growing army and French occupants of Vietnam went downhill, resulting in a war that was fought off and on for eight years. In the spring of 1954, at a remote mountain village called Dien Bien Phu, Ho's army finally defeated the French forces. The peace treaty signed that year in Geneva, Switzerland, ordered the French to leave. But it also split Vietnam into two countries again,

North Vietnam and South Vietnam. Most North Vietnamese were communists, while the South Vietnamese claimed more interest in democracy.

Those who ran South Vietnam promised elections to reunite the country. When they delayed the elections, the North Vietnamese sent trained fighters into the south. These people came to the villages and spoke out against South Vietnam's government. To remain in power, South Vietnamese officials asked for military aid from the United States.

US soldiers came to South Vietnam in the early 1960s to train people as soldiers; terrorism in the south soon increased dramatically. United States soldiers began to die alongside the Vietnamese. Gradually, thousands of US soldiers became involved in terrible fighting. South Vietnam's leaders, supported by the United States, also enlisted military help from Australia, the Philippines, South Korea, and Thailand.

As the war progressed, North Vietnam sent many troops south. They hiked for hundreds of miles down the jungle-covered Ho Chi Minh Trail. These troops gained a lot of support from rural people in the south. Southerners who turned against their own government became known as Viet Cong.

The United States brought modern weapons to fight in this very backward country. The Soviet Union and China supplied the north with equally deadly tools of warfare. Even though the US eventually dropped more bombs on Vietnam than were used in World War II, the Communists never stopped fighting. Perhaps they fought harder than people in the south because no soldiers of other nations fought alongside them.

America Departs

Many US citizens and soldiers in the field grew to hate the war. They demanded a change in US policy. Citizens staged rallies and peace protests as a sign of their disapproval of the war effort. In 1968, US president Lyndon B. Johnson announced that he would stop bombing Vietnam and reduce the number of soldiers in that country. By 1973, the last US combat soldier had left.

Now, winning or losing was up to the South Vietnamese. Even though North Vietnam's leader, Ho Chi Minh, had died in 1969, the northerners fought very hard. They were led by such long-time revolutionaries as Vo Nguyen Giap, the general who defeated the French in 1954. The south fell to northern forces in 1975. The two countries were quickly reunited — but at a terrible price. Some two million Vietnamese had died in the war. Many more were injured, disabled, or even poisoned by chemicals.

Since the end of the war, Vietnam has faced many problems. As a result of heavy bombing, the landscape suffered terrible damage, and the Vietnamese people have struggled to produce enough food. Cities destroyed during the war had to be rebuilt without technological know-how or adequate funding. The ruins of war confront the Vietnamese every day, even after all these years.

Today, Vietnam is one of the poorest countries on earth. Bomb craters mark much of the land. Piles of junk from the war are left to rust and rot. Streams, canals, forests, and farmlands are terribly polluted. Health care varies widely from place to place. The Communist government so far has been unable to solve the country's many problems.

Government

Today's Vietnamese citizens don't have much say in the Communist national policy. But each village does have its own council to help decide minor judicial matters. In addition, the 35 provinces (states) and three major cities — Hanoi, Ho Chi Minh City (formerly Saigon), and Hai Phong — are each run by an elected people's council.

The national government is run by a prime minister who is elected from a Council of Ministers. Each of these ministers is in charge of a department responsible for a specific matter, such as education or defense. The ministers are named to their posts by the National Assembly. The National Assembly is elected by all Vietnamese adults who choose to vote. Members come from throughout Vietnam. In theory, their duties are similar to those of the US Congress or the Canadian Parliament — they create laws, discuss the well-being of the nation, and try to spend the country's money wisely.

Yet the National Assembly is less important than the Communist party. Communist leaders at all levels of government, headed by a national party chairperson, make sure that Vietnam sticks to party beliefs. They often hold political discussions in villages and neighborhoods after working hours. Anyone 18 or over is encouraged to join the Communist party. But the party is less popular than it once was because it has not been able to solve Vietnam's economic woes.

Since Vietnam is a communist country, the government controls the economy and runs all the industries. In some instances, small-scale private enterprise is allowed as long as the people involved continue to meet their Communist party responsibilities. Many Vietnamese also have two jobs in order to make extra money.

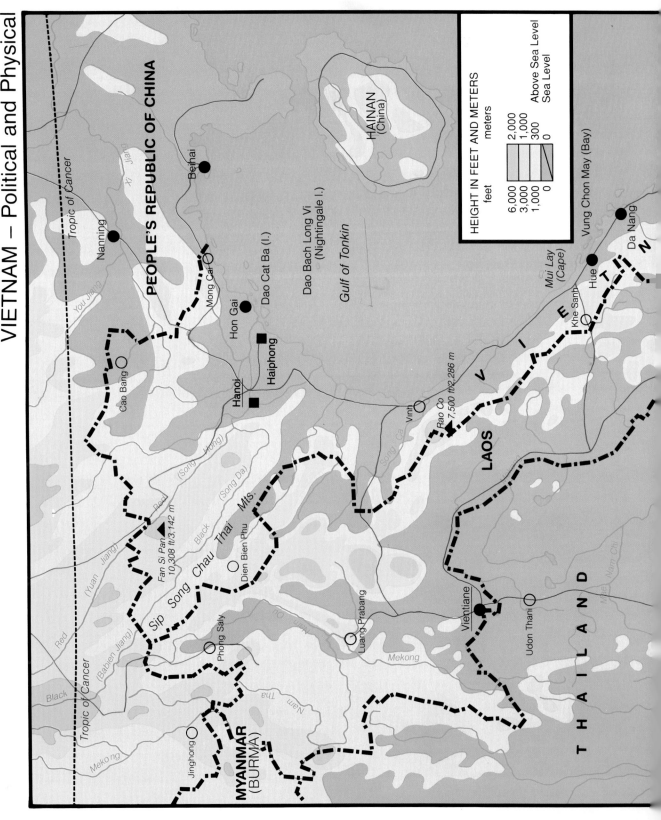

VIETNAM – Political and Physical

PEOPLE'S REPUBLIC OF CHINA

HEIGHT IN FEET AND METERS
feet   meters

6,000   2,000
3,000   1,000   Above Sea Level
1,000   300
0   0   Sea Level

Tropic of Cancer

Nanning

Beihai

Mong Cai

Hon Gai

Dao Cat Ba (I.)

Dao Bach Long Vi
(Nightingale I.)

Gulf of Tonkin

HAINAN
(China)

Cao Bang

Haiphong

Hanoi

Red

Yuan Jiang

You Jiang

Xi Jiang

Red
(Song Hong)

Black
(Song Da)

Fan Si Pan
10,308 ft/3,142 m

Sip Song Chau Thai Mts.

Dien Bien Phu

Black
(Babien Jiang)

Tropic of Cancer

Black

Mekong

Jinghong

MYANMAR
(BURMA)

Nam Tha

Nam Ou

Phong Saly

Luang Prabang

Mekong

Song Ca

Vinh

Rao Co
7,500 ft/2,286 m

LAOS

Vientiane

Udon Thani

THAILAND

Mae Nam Chi

Khe Sanh

Mui Lay
(Cape)

Vung Chon May (Bay)

Hue

Da Nang

V I E T N A M

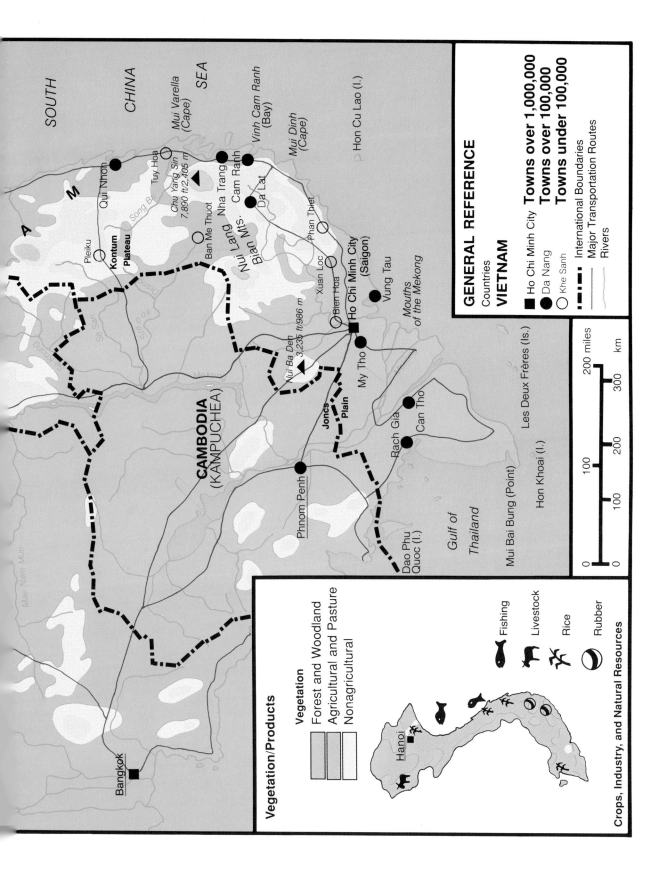

SOUTH CHINA SEA

CHINA

Mui Varella (Cape)

Qui Nhon

Tuy Hoa

Chu Yang Sin
7,890 ft/2,405 m

Ban Me Thuot

Nha Trang

Cam Ranh

Vinh Cam Ranh (Bay)

Mui Dinh (Cape)

Da Lat

Pleiku

Kontum Plateau

Nui Lang Bian Mts.

Hon Cu Lao (I.)

Phan Thiet

Xuan Loc

Bien Hoa

Ho Chi Minh City (Saigon)

3,235 ft/986 m

Vung Tau

Mouths of the Mekong

Nui Ba Den

My Tho

Joncs Plain

Rach Gia

Can Tho

Phnom Penh

CAMBODIA (KAMPUCHEA)

Gulf of Thailand

Hon Khoai (I.)

Mui Bai Bung (Point)

Les Deux Frères (Is.)

Dao Phu Quoc (I.)

Bangkok

A N N A M

Song Ba

Se San

Sre Pok

Mekong

Mae Nam Mun

Srepok

Darlac

Vegetation/Products

Vegetation
▨ Forest and Woodland
▨ Agricultural and Pasture
☐ Nonagricultural

🐟 Fishing
🐄 Livestock
🌾 Rice
◑ Rubber

Hanoi

Crops, Industry, and Natural Resources

Land and Climate

Think of the letter s. That is the shape of Vietnam, a long, thin country stretching more than 1,000 miles (1,600 km) along the western edge of the South China Sea. Its northern neighbor is China. To the west are Laos and Cambodia (formerly Kampuchea). Neighbors across the sea include the Philippines to the east and Malaysia and Indonesia to the south.

A backbone of mountains runs down the middle of the country. In the north and south, the land flattens out. These delta areas were created by mighty rivers, the Red in the north and the Mekong in the south. The Mekong, one of the world's longest rivers, begins hundreds of miles to the northwest, in the Himalaya Mountains of Tibet. Vietnam's mountains aren't as high as the Himalayas; in fact, they never see snow. The tallest peak is just 10,000 feet (3,050 m). But the barren or forested hills are alive with mosquitoes, snakes, and other creatures. For months each year, fog and rain wrap themselves around the mountains and cover the many remote valleys.

Monsoon winds bring rainy weather to Vietnam. Because different monsoons blow at different times of the year, the weather changes from one end of the country to the other. In the north, winters tend to be cool and rainy, with hot and dry summers. In the south, winters are dry and warm and summers are wet and hot. The heaviest rains fall on the country's narrow middle. The city of Hue, for instance, gets about 116 inches (294 cm) of rain each year. Occasional typhoons (tropical storms) are dangerous in coastal areas.

Vietnam's 127,242 square miles (329,557 sq km) make it about as big as New Mexico, or half the size of Alberta. The country narrows to less than 50 miles (80 km) at its middle and has more than 2,000 miles (3,200 km) of coastline. Many beaches line the coast, along with thick mangrove swamps and rocky islands.

The huge lowland growing areas in the north and south produce big crops of rice. Their rich, black soil is renewed every year when farmers let the muddy rivers overflow their rice paddies. Most of the rest of the country has poor soil, although rubber and fruit trees are common.

Agriculture and Industry

Before the war, Vietnam grew enough rice to feed itself and other countries, too. But the war destroyed much of the farming in the countryside. Only recently have rice farmers again grown enough for their own people. Besides rice, commercial crops include potatoes, sweet potatoes, corn, manioc, and sugarcane. Rubber trees on plantations ooze creamy sap that is sent overseas for car tires and other products. Farmers grow and export crops such as flowers and strawberries in the highlands. Fishing provides the Vietnamese with their most important source of protein.

Foreign money, often from the Soviet Union or Japan, has helped Vietnam create a few industries. They include fertilizer factories, chemical plants, cement works, plastics factories, bicycle factories, food-processing plants, and cotton, steel, and paper mills.

Natural Resources

Except for coal, Vietnam has only a few natural resources of commercial value. Those resources include apatite, bauxite, chromate, iron, phosphate, and manganese. Also, the search is on for oil off Vietnam's coast. Forests that survived the war and cover approximately 40% of the land yield valuable hardwoods. But much of the soil is poor, its nutrients having been washed away over centuries of seasonal rains.

Education

Schooling is free for 12 years and is funded by the national government. But not everyone can afford to stay in school that long, since boys and girls often help their parents farm or work in market stalls. School buildings are sometimes no more than blackboards set up under a tin roof supported by poles. But learning is important to the Vietnamese, almost all of whom can read. According to the most recent statistics, an estimated 94% of Vietnam's population is literate.

Schools are crowded because Vietnam's Communist government has little money either for constructing new classrooms or for purchasing necessary educational supplies. Also, huge numbers of young children have started school, since the relatively small number of Vietnamese who survived the war seemed determined to rebuild the population. In the years following the end of the Vietnam conflict, there was a population explosion. School days are divided into two sessions in many areas throughout the country so that as many children as possible can go to school. Morning sessions begin early and end around noon five or six days a week. Then, different children and a different group of teachers show up for school during the afternoon. Vacations center around seasonal work in the rice paddies and around Tet, the Vietnamese New Year holiday. Vietnam has three universities and more than 40 colleges and technical schools.

Religion

Not all Vietnamese are religious, but many seem to be superstitious. Many have faith, for example, in geomancy. This is an ancient belief that everything should line up in its proper place or direction. So great care is taken in planning which direction a building faces or where a grave is dug.

Other religious influences include Taoism and Confucianism. Both are ancient Chinese beliefs that include ancestor worship and rules about proper ways to behave. These beliefs influence the country's leading religion, Buddhism. Buddhism began in India about 500 BC. It teaches that each person should try to reach a condition beyond suffering or existence.

A large minority of the population practices Roman Catholicism. There are several other minor religions, such as Cao Dai, which mixes many religious beliefs and features a Christian-style church in the city of Tay Ninh adorned with dragons! Many hill tribes practice animism — the belief that everything has a soul, even objects such as rocks and trees.

Population and Ethnic Groups

Vietnam's population in 1990 was about 68 million. Four of every five Vietnamese live in rural areas, although both rural and urban areas show signs of overpopulation. Lack of housing, overcrowded schools, and food shortages are just a few problems that plague the country's people.

About 85% of all citizens are native Vietnamese. They are descended from farmers who lived in southern China thousands of years ago. The rest are Chinese, Khmer, Meo, Thai, or one of dozens of hill-tribe minorities.

Minorities in Vietnam have not fared well since the war ended. Many city dwellers of Chinese heritage were branded as enemies by Soviet Communists. Hill tribes that refused to join cooperative farms or remained pro-French were threatened or chased into Laos. Children whose mothers were Vietnamese and whose fathers were US soldiers suffered from neglect. No wonder thousands have risked their lives to flee Vietnam in recent years.

Language

Almost everyone speaks Vietnamese, although some words and the ways in which they are pronounced differ between north and south. A few older people still speak a Chinese dialect in the home. But Chinese is heard less often these days, since 140,000 people of Chinese descent have fled Vietnam in the last 15 years. Hill tribes have their own languages, some of which have never been written. English, French, and Russian are popular languages in public schools. Students decide which language they want to learn when they are at the elementary grade level.

The Vietnamese language is tonal. That means that a simple word like *ma* can have six different meanings, depending on how it is pronounced! While English-speaking North Americans usually talk in a constant tone of voice, Vietnamese run their voices up and down the scale, somewhat like singing.

Culture

Many countries have tried to impose their own cultures on Vietnamese culture. The Chinese alphabet, the Soviet political system of communism, French architecture, and United States consumer products are just a few examples. Despite this influx of outside influences, however, the Vietnamese have managed to develop and maintain their own culture. It can be seen in graceful designs painted on silk or woven into cotton cloth. It can be heard in songs that are ancient Vietnamese poems set to music. It can be seen in the pottery, paintings, and shiny lacquerware sold throughout the country. And it can almost be felt in air thick with smoky incense inside a colorful temple.

Manners matter a great deal in Vietnam. Even the poorest and least educated rural resident is expected to treat older people with politeness and respect, to cooperate in whatever tasks may be assigned, and to be a law-abiding member of the community. The Vietnamese people point out that their country may be poor, but centuries of tradition also give it a quiet and powerful dignity.

Sports

The average Vietnamese has little or no time or energy for sports. For example, people go fishing to get food for the family rather than for recreation. Vietnamese with time to spare are more likely to do repairs or scavenge than they are to play a sport or game.

Those fortunate enough to have leisure time often play racket games like tennis or badminton. Bicycling is popular, and so are soccer and track and field events. Swimming at one of the country's many beaches can be done all year round in southern and central Vietnam.

Currency

The *dong* is Vietnam's unit of currency. It is very difficult to know just how much the dong is worth in US currency at any one time because of high inflation in Vietnam. Estimates claim that exchange rates can vary from 80 to 5,000 dong per US dollar, and even this figure constantly changes.

Vietnamese money before North and South Vietnam were reunified.

Hanoi

Dropped into the middle of Hanoi, a stranger might think he or she was in 19th-century France. The faded, peeling buildings are of French design, and so are the ancient streetcars. But a closer look would reveal not only Oriental faces and a few modern conveniences such as radios, but also the smell of Vietnamese food with strong sauces made of fish, soy, garlic, peppers, lemon grass, and other ingredients.

Hanoi has hardly any cars. The trucks and buses are old and in bad repair. The city is thick with bicycles, making the occasional motor scooter appear very fast in comparison. More than two million people live here, although the city's failure to maintain adequate living accommodations for its people makes it seem almost like a large, overgrown village.

Vietnamese in North America

More than 165,000 Vietnamese have become US citizens since the war ended in 1975. Entire neighborhoods of Vietnamese have sprung up in various places, such as Houston, Dallas, Washington, San Diego, Los Angeles, and San Francisco. Canadian cities such as Toronto and Vancouver also have new residents from Vietnam. Some immigrants live among the general population and have become very westernized.

More Books about Vietnam

Vietnam. Coley (Chelsea House)
Vietnam. Wright (Childrens Press)
The War in Vietnam. Lawson (Franklin Watts)
War in Vietnam (4 vols.) Wright (Childrens Press)

Glossary of Important Terms

apatite ....a type of mineral sometimes used to make fertilizer.

communism .....a political system based on the idea that the people of a country as a whole rather than individuals should own the wealth, property, businesses, and industries of that country. Ideally, communism's goal is to distribute wealth evenly and provide for everyone's needs.

democracy ......a government ruled by the people. Citizens in a democracy usually elect representatives to vote on important issues.

hangar ....a large, covered building usually used to store airplanes and helicopters.

monsoon ....a strong wind bringing heavy rains to parts of the world.

Glossary of Useful Vietnamese Terms

ba (bah) ....three
cha (chah) ....father
chao (chow) ....hello; good-bye
con gai (KAWN guy) ....girl
con trai (KAWN try) ....boy
hai (hi) ....two
lua (LOO-ah) ....rice
me (meh) ....mother
mot (moat) ....one
truong (TROO-uhn) ....school

Things to Do — Research Projects and Activities

Although Vietnam is a poor country, the people who live there value education. They are working to solve their economic problems by training young people to use the resources that are available. The Vietnamese are a strong people, made stronger by centuries of tradition and personal dignity.

The following research projects might help you understand some of the important issues in Vietnam. For accurate, up-to-date information, you may have to go to the nearest library. Ask for one or both of the following publications, which will have listings of recent articles on many topics. Look up *Vietnam* in these two publications:

Readers' Guide to Periodical Literature
Children's Magazine Guide

1. Vietnam is one of the poorest countries on earth. How did the many years of conflict there make the country poor? How did the different forms of government help or hinder the economy? What does Vietnam's economic future look like?

2. The Vietnamese are a mixture of different peoples. With a map of Southeast Asia, try to find paths ancestors of the Vietnamese may have followed to reach modern Vietnam. Consider problems caused by mountains, oceans, jungles, and weather.

3. The average Vietnamese is much younger than the average European or North American. Why is this so? Will a large, young population be a help or a hindrance for the country in the future? Why or why not?

4. How far is Vietnam from where you live? Which country is closer to the equator? To the Tropic of Cancer? To the Tropic of Capricorn? How many time zones away from your home is Vietnam?

5. Compare Chau's life to your own. Discuss the ways in which they are the same or different.

6. If you would like a pen pal in Vietnam, write to:

   International Pen Friends
   P.O. Box 290065
   Brooklyn, NY 11229

   Worldwide Pen Friends
   P.O. Box 39097
   Downey, CA 90241

   Be sure to tell them what country you want your pen pal to be from. Also include your full name, age, and address.

Kim Chau and her sisters say good-bye.

Index